Learn, Commit, Grow- with Personal Yoga

Have Fun in the Process

CAROLINA HERRERA
FLÓREZ

DEDICATION

Your breath, your mind and your body on and off the
mat. Have a fun time in your process.

This is for all yogis who want to have fun, and grow a
personal yoga practice.

CONTENTS

ACKNOWLEDGMENTS

I would like to express my gratitude to the many people who saw me through this book; to all those who provided support, talked things over, read, wrote, offered comments, allowed me to quote their remarks and assisted in the editing, proofreading and design.

"Communicating, moving and breathing on and off the mat- is an art of personal living" Carolina Herrera Flórez

1.   I AM MY HAPPY PLACE

I am Carolina Herrera and I was born in Bogota, Colombia. While we share a name, I am not the famous fashion designer. I am the personal yoga teacher and health coach expert, that has dedicated her life to learning about health and wellness. I grew up in a small faith-based community. As a child, contemplating how big the world is always kept my curious mind busy. I had the honor of learning a different language and had the privilege of being able to take a few trips with my family. Going on family vacations was very important to me growing up. I got to spend time with my loved ones doing what we did best: travelling and learning about different aspects of the world and places.

As a family we thoroughly enjoyed any kind of rides, be it by car, plane, horse, bike or boat. I remember though for me this was no easy task. My family, both mom and dad, seemed to have such fierce energy. To this day I admire them.

Getting up and going at 6 a.m. was never really an easy task for me. Eating healthy was not on my books, and being active was something I had to do just to be part of the family and travel. I can tell you this was not something I really enjoyed. In my teenage years, I went on to high school and was sent over to be an exchange student for my last year of high school to study abroad in Minnesota. Moving so far from home was my fierce 15-year-old choice, and I thank my parents for allowing me to experience it. I learned that what I knew about the world was only my version of it. Through this new lens, I learned how huge the world is. This is the first time I remember being confused by how big the world really is. This opened my horizon and allowed me to learn about the opportunities that another country could hold for me.

I decided to stay in the United States and learn. I diligently worked through Nursing School, graduated and got a few jobs that led me to the path I am currently on. After working in the health industry for over a decade, I understand three key things. 1. Wellness 2. Yoga 3. What does science say about yoga?

Wellness.

Wellness guides my understanding of what I have to plan on a daily basis to help me achieve an optimal level of functioning. (This can range from financial, emotional, physical wellness) Every day, every year, things are different and will be as I continue the humanly aging process.

Yoga.

I came into contact with this spiritual Hindu practice as it started to pop up commercially at different studios about 12 years ago. I lived in Minnesota at the time, and because of the long , cold winters I joined a few hot yoga studios. I loved the way I felt after each visit, which started my interest in yoga.

I wasn't the person I am now 12 years ago. At the start of my nursing career I was 30 pounds heavier than I am now, and I smoked. I was away from my family, living in a different country, getting used to cold weather, so I was not well.

I am thankful that I was able to recognize all the positive things that stood with me. I always looked for support and I joined a wonderful health club. I was social and surrounded myself with people. I have had the pleasure of meeting hundreds and hundreds of people, and I can tell you that not a single one has ever declined to help me in some significant way. This is to acknowledge all the families that brought me under their wing, providing me with a home and a family to be part of . During my educational process, I received scholarships and awards that made going to school a possibility. Somehow I made it with all the support from really kind and amazing people who are friends and will always be there. One thing I have told myself and will continue to tell myself is I have one body and one life and I am here to make the most of it. So now I share my passion for wellness through the ancient Hindu practice of yoga as well as writing, podcasts, and wherever else this passion takes me. If you want to personally work with me, please reach out as I'm always happy to help.

2.   PRESENTS

I currently manage my time to create a fun project –.
Over the past year, I have dedicated at least two hours
a day to learning about yoga. I realize my journey is
long as there is much to learn about the Hindu
tradition. I am now doing virtual 10-minute
personalized practices and coaching to include the
practice each day. I never really thought I could be an
author, though. This is a really fun way to show you
what I mean by including a personal practice. And
here I am- stretching myself off the mat and – writing
you a book.

The practice of yoga and any other exercise form that
is enjoyable to you now is a personal lifelong project.
You age and things will be different at every stage. All
you can do is support your body by establishing a
mindful regular connection with your mind and body
through the movement of yoga asanas. I aim to
understand more about the cultural aspects of the
yoga tradition to inspire me to live a life with plenty
of opportunities to explore wellness at many different
levels. I see yoga as a practice and cultural tradition I

am really inclined to learn about. But, let's face it, I did not grow up with the tradition. What I aim to do is take that information and translate into a possible application in my life in a way that works, and repeat all over again, and share with the world. I remain curious about what yoga is and see it as a cultural aspect of the Hindu tradition that provides me with a tool for practicing breathing with movement. In my youth, I seldom had the time to take a breather, or a zenful 10 minutes of my own. Typically, when you take 10 minutes, this has a bad connotation. You either use them to cool off from a stressful situation, or you are in the real stressful situation all day and never take the time to decompress. The main fact that drives my yoga practice is that I know one thing is real: 10 minutes of personal yoga practice leaves me refreshed and provides me with the opportunity to move my body mindfully. This is an opportunity that I can give to the body to enjoy 10 minutes every day. If you typically go to a yoga class at least once or twice a week, then this is for you. If you are with a yogi practicing regularly and want to have a class with me any time, then this is for you. I add value to your yogic practice by having an additional touchpoint of overall health and wellness from my nursing experience, creating a truly holistic approach to yoga.

3. FUN PERSONAL YOGA

I am here to share with you, ongoing fun tools to practice breathing and moving and create a practice that your body is thankful for. I hope to guide you into learning about becoming involved in the art of moving and breathing and creating Zen in your life. I will craft programs to teach you tools, and connect you with many other influencers to continue to grow your Zen at every level. Your practice is your best practice.

I encourage going to other practices and other studios. This is must for learning about yoga and personal growth. Together in my community we will be able to discuss the best tools and what they are for. I hope to connect with others in my profession and continue to learn more about the scientific effects of yoga in the human body.

4. A BEGINNER MINDSET IN YOGA

Have you ever read sayings telling you to live your legend, do what you like, be your own? If this resonates with you, then I am very glad you are here, and that you are willing to explore what beginnings should look like. Embarking on new activities is not only fun, but it adds to your personal journey. Have you ever travelled to a place and returned more energized? Have you ever been proud of yourself? If so, great! Congratulations for doing the initial work to recognize that you have skills, you are creative and therefore able to achieve what you had hoped for. Big goals and big dreams always start off small.

When you embark in the process of learning something new you can come up with thousands of alternatives, and you might try to talk yourself out of the task at hand as it takes you out of your comfort zone. This is a cycle that can only be understood if you wear that beginner's hat.

In yoga, it does not matter how long you have practiced because you will always be a beginner. You are inclined to always step onto your mat with the mindset of a beginner. This is really what matters when building a personal practice.

Your beginner mindset is to learn about your breathing, while you are moving through the asanas that the ancient Hindu tradition has slowly emerged as yoga in the Western hemispheres. A beginner's mindset is crucial to stepping onto your mat with the ability to create 10 minutes or more of fun personal flow with yourself in mind. What do you like to do when you focus on your breathing? Would you do this after your walk, after your run, before your massage, before bedtime, before a meeting, after a conference, inside, outside, with music, with out music? Will you use one breath to one movement or five breaths in one asana? The opportunities are as endless as the benefits.

Daily yoga asana practice will improve your muscle flexibility and strength. This mindful approach to moving your body to your breathing will also increase the awareness of your body, therefore your posture may improve. Yoga is a low impact form of activity for your body and safe when practiced under the guidance of a teacher of your choosing. Always consult with your well-trained yoga teacher before starting a practice-. If you have any health concerns, please discuss this with your doctor prior to beginning a daily yoga practice.

Do not use yoga to replace conventional medicine. Always consult with your doctor, and share how many classes you do each week. You should also specify whether it is hot yoga, commercial yoga, Youtube yoga, or better yet if you are working with a personal trainer or personal yoga teacher. Discuss any benefits or areas of concern so everyone involved can learn more about your body and treat it safely.

Yoga comprises physical, mental, and spiritual practices from India. As the practice continues to grow, you may also be inclined to learn about the yogic lifestyle. I will teach you more about the yogi lifestyle in future books

.

5. LEARN

Learning is a process. The most important aspect of learning in yoga is that you remain open to exploring the ability that you have to focus on your breathing and move accordingly and make your movement be a fun memorable experience that you love. Learning in yoga starts with learning about your breath. How do you catch yourself when you are not focused at breathing in an asana? Ideally, you will do it with compassion, and then you do it all over again, get focused on your breath and move again.

This learning phase is probably the hardest one. Wanting to learn is likely the last reason you initially step onto your mat. Learning, though, makes sense. When your mind is relaxed and focused on the breath there is really nothing to learn other than to keep the practice going. The learning component comes after the practice: What did you gain? How do you feel? Ask your self whether it is worth the 10 minutes.

If your answer was yes, then you may have been learning about yourself, learning about your breath, and how the mind and the body connect. You are cultivating a mindful approach to learning about yoga and about yourself.

6. COMMIT

This is your declaration, you are going to practice your personal yoga every day.

Tips for staying committed

1. Establish three different times that you think are the best parts of the day.
    Identify your personal favorite and why. Because you need to plan for the best part of your day, ponder about the smells, scenery and music you like. These will add to your beginner flow. Then choose one and do your personal flow.
2. Identify why you are practicing. Is it to practice meditation? Or, perhaps you want to learn about your breath? Are you interested in yoga asanas and what your body has to accomplish before it gets there? Or, do you simply love how you feel after practicing yoga? The reason is yours and only yours, so I am assuming it is very important. Therefore, making the best of your 10 minutes is

probably the best thing you can do for yourself each day.

3. Use calendar reminders: Let's face it, breathing on a mat is probably ranked low on your daily to-do list. So, being mindful of a time and creating a commitment to it will serve you the purpose of creating a space for the practice on a busy day.

4. Have your yoga teacher be your guide: Request a virtual or telephonic visit with me and I will be happy to be your guide.

5. Go to group yoga sessions: It is important to me as your yoga teacher that you continue attending other classes. I suggest at least one each week so you can learn from other types of yoga. It is important to establish connections with others and share the practice and the breath in one room.

7. GROW

Yoga is about stretching, moving and learning. Requesting feedback on successes or failures is really the only way to grow.

The process of feedback

1. Understand and perform your yoga as planned: Have an appointment on your schedule and use your tracking device to monitor heart, breathing and time.

2. The use of personalized devices to help you track yourself will help you remain consistent with the result-oriented mentality and live a yogic life. Pick a moment of your week or day to log into your fitness device and monitor progress.

3. Congratulate yourself for all the successes, and note areas where you can still grow. Ask for guidance or further feedback that will help you continue to improve.

4. Check in with your yoga peeps- trainers.

5. The most important: HAVE FUN IN THE PROCESS. Asses the areas that need work, get

creative and make the process work for you.

8. YOUR LEGACY

What I learned at 15

I was 15 years old when I left my house, my parents, my family, my friends, teachers, country and everything familiar to me to go to a country where I didn't speak the language. Why? I am not entirely sure. The country I lived in at the time I left was not doing well and I felt unsafe every day. I always wondered if the grass was really greener on the other side, so at 15 my dad offered me a deal. Do you want a quinceañera or would you rather pick a place and go somewhere? Both options were very enticing. I did have a lot of friends who at the time were all turning 15 and we had a quinceañera almost every weekend. While I thought those parties were really fun, I never thought I really wanted one for myself. Instead, I chose option two and picked somewhere to go. Please send me to Paris, Europe, the U.S., essentially around the globe, I said. My father's reply wasn't quite as glamorous. He said I could live with his cousin for one year in Minnesota and wouldn't negotiate further.

That was my very first visit to Minnesota. I remember saying my goodbyes and crying with family and friends who I would miss dearly. I boarded the plane and to my surprise, the weather was so cold I couldn't move. I was wearing a jacket and some gloves my mom had made for me but it was still cold. I think that impact broke my internal thermostat, and I wanted to jump back in the plane and return to the tropical land of Colombia where I came from. But at that point it was too late. That was a no go. I had to stay.

The impact of the new culture and new experiences was a bittersweet deal. I got to experience real cold weather for the first time in my life. Then I started to realize all the differences in food, Minnesota is rich in lakes and has a lovely community. I made friends, learned English and decided to go back after one year to finish high school in Colombia. I did, and after a year I was back as an exchange student with bigger goals in mind.

Someone once told me that hardship creates personality. I think for me the realization of understanding my passion for travel has inspired my life choices, and my love for moving and learning.

My story draws many parallels to yoga. Yoga looks fun and yoga teachers move with such ease standing on their heads and twisting like pretzels. Their bodies seem easy and healthy to handle. As you step onto the mat you probably think that the last thing you are there to do is to learn about you. As the class starts the yoga teacher begins talking and kindly guide the asanas, and suddenly everyone is moving and breathing. The result is beautiful. Everyone is in thought, focusing on whatever the practice brings to them. After the practice, or during the practice, you learn to connect your mind, breath and movement.

This is hard to do, but with practice and dedication anything is possible. As a child I learned that I wanted to be able to move and travel, and to this day I am grateful I chose to travel at a young age. Your personal yoga practice teaches you about yourself. Relax and enjoy, while you are here committing to grow your personal yoga zen time.

I offer a 10 week online personal yoga class- (PYC) on learning about a personal yoga practice, tailored to you. I am here to empower you to step onto your mat and start working on your legacy.

Go to www.magentastars.com and buy your class.

9. A WORK IN PROGRESS

Adapting at 15 years of age seemed easier. As the years go by, comfort starts to set in and people get set in their ways. You develop a sweet comfort zone, that zone in which you sit and life is beautiful and days go by.

I think back to my earlier years. When I worked in hospitals I realized that life is precious. A hospital is a place of endurance, both for the patients and the health team. I started my career in hospitals as a certified nursing assistant working long hours. I was amongst the happiest workers. I remember going into the hospital every day, and staying committed to serving. Serving can be exhausting passion. At this point, I was in my twenties I was fluent in English and was able to live on my own. I had been committed to my development fully, yet I had much more to discover. Even though I knew that serving in a hospital is hard work, takes dedication and it is exhausting- the commitment of showing up serving and learning was still there. I remember the long hours of nursing school and the adrenaline, because all of it was exciting and rewarding, and at the same time exhausting.

I found that it is important to understand why staying committed to something is worth the time, the hardship and the effort. To me it is really important to give back, and being a part of the health care team in a hospital or at my current position within the health team seem like the perfect way to give back. After all, I have been adopted by this society and healing and supporting healing is the only way of giving back. My profession in nursing has allowed me to see humanity unfold in front of my eyes. I understand hardships. As a nurse, I am trained to evaluate the airway-breathing, pulse, blood pressure, to establish a baseline functioning and then monitor any ups or downs, and work with a team.

In life I am trained to be flexible, adapt to change and learn as much as I can from experiences to adapt accordingly. Breathing is the kind act that we humans do to our bodies so they stay functioning. Oxygen is our source of energy to live. If you are breathing, you are alive.

I understand I don't need to be in a hospital to tell you about your breathing. I went on to get additional leisure education on yoga, an aspect I am committed to continue to grow on. Yoga is about breathing. It is about moving your body with your breath. This simple act of getting and staying committed to a practice or a hobby is worth the effort.

Staying committed can be a difficult task to accomplish and I can be there to assist in the process of recognizing how important moving and breathing is and how it adds zen to your life.

10 TECHNOLOGY AND PERSONAL YOGA

Let's discuss virtual yoga and how we are here. When I started learning about yoga informally, I would have never guessed that I would stretch myself to teach yoga and share knowledge. Initially, I only went to classes for my benefit. I started taking yoga classes as the new form of fitness that was slowly growing in my community. Yoga was that feel-good sport I practiced after my biking, hiking, running, walking and skating. I would practice and be really good about practicing, but like with most hobbies, they come and go or I would get bored, or not show up for weeks at a time or even months until I'd pick it up again.

I found myself one summer at a yoga studio dear to my heart. That day was an inspiring one. After a long day of work, going to yoga was the ultimate highlight of my day.

One day after class, one of the yoga teachers started talking about why she practiced yoga and invited fellow community members to become yoga teachers to deepen our own practice and to grow to be committed to it. This really resonated with me since I already knew how easy to forget yoga was for me. So, I signed up and over that summer I stayed committed. My summer consisted of 200 hours of memorable hot yoga moments on the mat. It was then that I realized how much growth there is to journey through.

As a yoga teacher and as a nurse, I always try to balance my days so that they are enjoyable. I know that with my passion for health and wellness I am ready to commit to my personal yoga fun time. I am ready to merge yoga and wellness and serve someone that is looking to incorporate some personal safe yoga into their day. The perspective of being free to practice at the times it is convenient for myself depending on the day, understanding why I lead a practice and why I lead others to create their personal practice entices me. I struggled with this concept. I struggled to find my why. I pondered my reason for practicing and wanting to share. One day I started research to see how I could connect with individuals of my same school of thought. I discovered tools that sparked my creativity and now I can say that I have successfully taught individuals who have used yoga asanas to include at least 10 minutes of personal yoga practice. I can tell you that this is the most rewarding experience yet. I see some of my clients have had successes and failures and continue to remain fully immersed in their personal learning, commitment and growth.

A special thanks for all the support I received while writing and for the inspiration from all of you yogis. This book, my work and my dedication is for you.

Namaste

ABOUT THE AUTHOR

Carolina approaches yoga as her personal time to explore breathing, moving, and establish a connection between her mind and body. She is known for her authentic, non-judgmental teaching style and her compassion-centered philosophy. She weaves a personalized practice throughout her classes because she draws from her continuous health-related work, wellness, and yoga therapy education from different schools. She encourages a safe yoga practice by working with a simple routine. For Carolina yoga is a tool that helps her learn at her own pace about working the body. She defines moving and breathing as very powerful tools when leading a healthy and balanced lifestyle.